Believe
IN WHAT YOU'RE DOING

BELIEVE
IN WHO YOU ARE

BELIEVE IN WHAT YOU'RE DOING
BELIEVE IN WHO YOU ARE

HILARY WEEKS

DESERET BOOK

SALT LAKE CITY, UTAH

© 2008 Hilary Weeks

Visit us at DeseretBook.com

Library of Congress Cataloging-in-Publication Data
Weeks, Hilary.
  Believe in what you're doing, believe in who you are / Hilary Weeks.
     p. cm.
  ISBN 978-1-59038-920-1 (hardcover : alk. paper)
  1. Mormon women—Religious life. 2. Weeks, Hilary. I. Title.
BX8641.W44 2008
248.8′43088289332—dc22   2008017380

Printed in Mexico
R. R. Donnelley and Sons, Reynosa, Mexico

10   9   8   7   6   5   4   3   2   1

Introduction

I HAVE NEVER WRITTEN A book. Oh wait, I take that back. Yes, I have; I was in second grade. It was a book about a little brown bear named Cuddles who got lost while picking flowers in the woods. I love happy endings, so Cuddles eventually found his way home. I hesitate to toot my own horn, but I was also the illustrator. If I do say so myself, the illustrations were almost as good as the story line.

Considering my illustrious career as an author, you might be surprised to know that when I was invited to write this book I felt unequal to the task. However, I accepted the challenge, and this is why: Everyone needs reminders. I don't know a single person who doesn't need a reminder now and then. That is why we have calendars, PDAs, laptops, alarm clocks, day planners, sticky notes, string to tie on our fingers. After all the reminders about appointments, meetings, carpools, and deadlines, there is one reminder we need most of all: God loves us. Inside each one of us is the need to know that Heavenly Father is aware of us, that He believes in us, and that He understands how hard we are trying.

Several years ago I was invited to write a song for an album specifically created for women. I was told that I could write about any topic I wanted. I looked around my house and saw the piled-up dishes, the baskets of laundry, and the scattered toys. Suddenly I knew what I would yearn to hear if Heavenly Father could sit with me for a while and talk. I wanted to be reassured that my efforts were making a difference, that I was doing a good job with my family, that I was becoming more like the Savior, and that I was following the course He wants me to follow. I wanted to be reminded that I was His daughter and that He loved me. So I wrote the song "Who You Are."

> *I know you wonder if you'll ever have a day*
> *Where the kids stay calm, the laundry's done,*
> *and the dishes are put away*
> *And sometimes you feel like your days are*
> *spent and gone*
> *And the question running through your mind*
> *is, "What have I gotten done?"*
> *And when you finally have a moment to*
> *slow down*
> *At the end of your day*
> *I know Father would say*
> *Believe in what you're doing*
> *Believe in who you are*
> *Hold tight to the truth that you're a daughter*
> *of God*
> *Believe in who you're becoming*
> *Believe in who you are*

It may seem simple—all the little things you
    do
But the lives you touch matter so much and
    there's no one else like you
And Father needs you to stand tall and faithful
Be all you can be
Oh, if you could see what He sees
You'd believe in what you're doing
You'd believe in who you are
So hold tight to the truth that you're a daugh-
    ter of God
Believe in who you're becoming
Believe in who you are
When it's hard to believe in yourself
And you feel like you're beginning to doubt
Remember
He believes in what you're doing
He believes in who you are
Don't lose sight of the truth that you're a
    daughter of God
He believes in who you're becoming
He believes in who you are

That song is a reminder. This book is another
reminder. Not a reminder of what you need to

do or what you should do. But a reminder that you are doing better than you might think.

My hope is that you will reflect on the experiences of your own life as you read a few of mine. Think of the discoveries you have made—both big and small—and allow them to shape who you are becoming. Trust what you've learned. Believe in what you know.

And on the days when you wonder if you'll ever be enough, remember: *He* believes in who you're becoming. *He* believes in who you are.

Unexpected Answers

*And verily I say unto you, whatsoever things ye shall
ask the Father in my name shall be given unto you.
Therefore, ask, and ye shall receive; knock, and it shall be
opened unto you; for he that asketh, receiveth; and unto
him that knocketh, it shall be opened.*
—3 Nephi 27:28–29

I'M NOT REALLY WHAT YOU would call a water person. I guess you could say that it's because I haven't had much experience waterskiing, boating, snorkeling, etc. But let's face it, the truth of the matter is I am in no hurry to wear a swimsuit.

On the other hand, my husband, Tim, loves the water. One summer Tim talked me into renting a Jet Ski and adventuring around a lake for the day. I agreed, but only after he agreed to the rules:

No going fast

No tipping us over

No crazy business

No breaking the rules

We got a babysitter for the baby; McKenzie, who was six years old, came with us. It was a beautiful day to be on the water. I mustered all my courage and climbed on the Jet Ski with Tim and McKenzie, and we started out around the lake.

It was really fun—at first. Then Tim got a little more courageous and broke the rules. He tipped us over. All three of us splashed into the water. After our life jackets brought us to the surface, we climbed back onto the Jet Ski. As I climbed on the back, something in the water caught my eye. It was bright pink. It was sinking! I wanted to know what it was, so I tried to catch it with my foot. No luck. I just watched as the pretty pink thing disappeared into the bottom of the lake.

Well, we were ready to ride again when Tim noticed he didn't have the key to the Jet Ski. "What does it look like?" I asked.

"It's a black key attached to a bright pink thing."

Oops.

I told Tim I was pretty sure we weren't getting it back.

Now what? We were stuck in the middle of the lake without any way of starting the Jet Ski. Yeah, great idea. Let's do this every summer. We waved to other Jet Skiers to get their attention. We tried to flag down ski boats, but they were too busy having fun. (They still had their keys.) No one noticed us. And then our silent prayers were answered. And as Heavenly Father so often does, He answered in an unexpected way.

That happened to me another time—
Heavenly Father surprised me by His answer.
(Don't worry, I'll come back to the other story.) I
had been invited to open for Michael McLean
during the *Forgotten Carols* tour. The only problem
was that I would be performing several nights for
thousands of people. So? What's the problem?
Well, I was terrified of performing. I had been
for years. Singing in front of people made me so
nervous that I would feel sick. I was constantly
on my knees begging for the Lord to help me get
through it and do a good job. He always helped
me and never seemed weary of my endless plead-
ings. And though I always survived performing,
the nervousness was relentless. The thought of
singing night after night was almost more than I
could face. Early in December, before the
Forgotten Carols tour began, I asked Tim for a
priesthood blessing. In the blessing I was told
that this opportunity was my *reward* for years of

diligent performing. *I'm sorry, I'm not sure I heard you correctly,* I thought. *Did you say "reward"?* Very unexpected.

A reward it was indeed. The more I performed, the less nervous I became. Because it was several nights in a row, I had time to gain confidence. Each night the nervousness subsided a little more. And now, believe it or not, I enjoy performing!

Heaven sure sends some wonderful and unexpected surprises!

Now, where was I? Oh, yes, stuck in the middle of the lake. The three of us sat on the Jet Ski wondering how many days we would float there until someone came to our rescue. Then we noticed an old fisherman in a green, rickety motorboat coming towards us. No, this couldn't be our knight in shining armor. There is no way his boat could drag us to shore. But where there is a will, there is a way. Turns out the fish weren't biting and the fisherman had noticed our plight. It took a good, long while, but we finally made it to shore.

Heavenly Father answered our prayers, as He always does. I learned the answer is not to run from our fears but to face our fears knowing the Lord is on our side. And that the answer may not always be the sleek ski boat. Sometimes the answer is the old motorboat.

Believe that We hears you and that each prayer that rises to heaven returns answered.

Written in Their Hearts

Being taught the doctrines and principles of the gospel in such a way that they penetrate deep into our hearts is a powerful retention tool. The gospel has to be in our hearts; it has to be inside of us, in our very center, our core. As the Apostle Paul teaches, the gospel must be "written not with ink, but with the Spirit of the living God; not in tables of stone, but in fleshy tables of the heart" (2 Corinthians 3:3).
—Susan W. Tanner[1]

ALASKA IS A GORGEOUS STATE. I grew up in Anchorage. The magnificent beauty of the oceans, wildlife, mountains, and forests is breathtaking. There is a highway outside of Anchorage along the coast. On one side of the road is the ocean, and on the other side, huge, rugged mountains. It is a beautiful drive. In the summertime you can see beluga whales feasting in the abundant inlet.

The area is called Cook Inlet. The tide comes in and out two times a day. This inlet has the second highest tides in the world. The tide comes in quick and high. The water is bitterly cold. And the shore is covered in mud flats. It's not a sandy beach like you'd probably imagine. When the tide rolls out, what's left is a coastline of mud.

This mud is like quicksand. If you walk on it, it stays firm for a minute and then it begins to jiggle and pull you in. First your feet sink. Then your legs. Before you can pull yourself out, it is up to your waist. And you can't get out. Then the tide comes back in, and you either drown or die of hypothermia. Wanna visit Alaska now? I will probably never get hired to write the Alaska tourism ads. . . .

One summer when I was home from college I was going through a difficult time, so my dad took me for a drive along the coast. We stopped to watch the whales and to talk. Then we noticed some teenagers playing on a small peninsula that jutted out from the shore. The tide was in and so the peninsula was nearly surrounded by water. We watched them explore for a while.

Then my dad asked me, "If one of those kids fell into the water and was still close to the shore, would you jump in and try to help?"

I answered quickly, "Yeah. I'm a good enough swimmer and the shore is close enough that I think I could help."

Then he asked, "Do you think I would jump in and help?"

I replied, "Yes, definitely. You're bigger and stronger than I am, so you could for sure help them."

Then the next question: "If they fell in and were pulled out farther into the ocean, then would you jump in and help them?"

This time, I thought a little longer about my answer. "No. The water is so cold I could get hypothermia in minutes. And the tide is too swift—even boats can't navigate these waters. I would want to help, but I'm not strong enough."

"Do you think I would help?"

Again, I contemplated my answer. I said, "You're bigger than me. You're stronger than me. But, no, you couldn't help. The water is too cold and the waves too strong—even for you. And if you went in, it would just mean that two lives would be lost."

Then the final question. "If it was *you* that had fallen in and were being pulled out by the waves, do you think I would jump in and help?"

There was no doubt in my mind. Yes. I knew he would—because he's my dad. And I knew he loved me and he would do anything to help me. That's what he was trying to do that day—help me.

In an instant I also understood how much my Heavenly Father loved me.

I recently looked in my journal to see what I wrote about this experience, because I remember it so vividly.

I didn't write any of it.

The only thing I wrote on July 9, 1990, was how frustrated I was that my dad wanted to go for a drive. How annoyed I was by having to have a "talk." I expressed my resentment of the fact that *I* didn't express *my* feelings.

I was actually kind of shocked when I read that, because it is an experience I have looked back on so often. It reminded me of Enos and of how remembering the words of his father was a blessing in his life.

Sometimes it is hard to be sure that what we are teaching our children is making a difference or sinking in at all. But it is. Enos's father, Jacob, may have asked himself the same question—is anything I'm teaching this child making a difference at all? Is he hearing any of this? But Jacob didn't give up and neither should we. Because Jacob taught his son, there were words for Enos to recall and ponder when he needed it most.

Our family conversations and discussions can become a source of strength and comfort in future years. Our insight and direction will have a great impact on our posterity.

Believe that your conversations with your children may not be written in their journals, but they will be written in their hearts.

---

1. "Written in the Fleshy Tables of the Heart" Spring 2005 President's Message, found at lds.org/pa/display/0,17884,7037-1,00.html.

My Motto

The Lord endows us with confidence as we practice "charity towards all men" and have righteous thoughts. One way we can practice charity is to be generous in our praise of others, thus helping them gain confidence as well.
—Elder Glenn L. Pace[2]

HAVE YOU EVER FELT LIKE you didn't fit in? Or walked into a roomful of people and felt your insecurities were flashing in neon on your forehead? Have you ever avoided talking to people because you were worried about what they might think of you? Or have you decided that you'll never be given the award for "Most Confident"?

I remember a night when I was in charge of a Young Women's activity at the church. I don't remember what the activity was, but I'm sure it was spiritual, memorable, uplifting, engaging, exciting, and most likely spectacular. But then again, I don't have a very good memory.

I *do* remember during the activity I realized that I might be a nerd. I felt like one. It seemed that even though I wasn't much older than the young women, they thought I was old, ancient, just all-around not cool anymore. That was not a fun feeling. I wanted to be liked by the young women. I wanted them to think I was fun and hip. I was only twenty-four. It's not like I was collecting Social Security.

As I drove home I was feeling kind of bad about myself. Then the Spirit whispered a thought that has changed my life: *Don't worry about what others think of you. Worry about what they think of themselves when they are with you.*

I didn't need to concern myself with whether or not the young women thought I was important or valuable. I needed to make sure they felt that way about themselves.

Now when I talk with someone, I don't worry about whether or not they compliment me. I compliment them. I don't count how many questions they ask me as a measure of how well they like me. I think of engaging and interesting questions to ask them. I don't wait for a smile, I smile first. Focusing on others takes the worry away and helps me to be happy and confident. So I guess there is some truth to "Don't worry, be happy!"

Believe that as you look for the good in others, you'll find it in yourself.

---

2. "Confidence and Self-Worth," *Ensign,* Jan. 2005, 32.

Cinnamon and Scripture Study

Seek ye out of the best books
words of wisdom; seek learning, even
by study and also by faith.
—D&C 88:118

I HAVE NEVER BEEN TO Venezuela, but my brother, Mike, served his mission there. Mike and his companion had the opportunity to teach a family of three—a mom, a dad, and a daughter about four years old. The family was very poor. Their home consisted of four walls, five chairs, and a dirt floor. One day Mike and his companion went to teach the family in their home. There were just enough chairs for each of them to sit in one. My brother and his companion sat across from the family as they taught. After using his scriptures, Mike's companion placed them on top of the scripture case, which was sitting on the dirt floor. As the discussion continued, the little girl could not take her eyes off of the scriptures. She stared and stared at them. Finally she stood, picked up the scriptures, placed them on her chair, then sat down in the dirt.

She knew the scriptures were sacred. She wasn't old enough to read them, but somehow she sensed they were the word of God and deserved to be treated with respect.

I remember seeing my dad read the scriptures. He would sit in a comfortable chair in the corner of our living room. Seeing my dad study the scriptures inspired a desire in me to know more about them, and now I love studying the scriptures.

It hasn't always been easy to find time to devote to studying. It has been especially challenging as our family has grown. I have had to adjust my study time. Sometimes it has been in the evening after the kids have gone to bed. Sometimes it has been in the morning before they wake up. It changes depending on our family schedule. But I always try to make the time.

I can tell when I have skipped a few days of scripture study because I start to feel overwhelmed. When I read the scriptures regularly I feel empowered to accomplish everything that is on my plate. I am sustained by heaven's power. When I consistently take time to ponder the things I read and learn about the mysteries of God, I feel inspired. I have ideas for songs; I know how to respond to my family; I feel I'm led by the Holy Ghost. Opening our scriptures opens our hearts and minds to the promptings of the Spirit.

I don't have a very good memory and I sometimes forget the things I read, so I keep a little notebook in my scripture case. I write down the things I learn so I won't forget them and so Heavenly Father will know I value what He teaches me.

My husband, Tim, owns his own company. There are many advantages of owning your own business, but there are also many challenges to be met. For many months I had worried about a new online store that Tim was starting. Would it be successful? Would it provide for our needs? How long until we would bring home a paycheck? These questions filled my mind with doubt.

One morning as I was studying in the Book of Mormon, I followed a footnote that took me to the Doctrine and Covenants. In section 67 was a direct message to me from Heavenly Father. Verse two reads: "Behold and lo, mine eyes are upon you, and the heavens and the earth are in mine hands, and the riches of eternity are mine to give."

I was comforted that He was watching over us and our business and that He has the power to help us succeed. God is in charge, and I was reminded that He would provide.

Then I read verse three: "Ye endeavored to believe that ye should receive the blessing which was offered unto you; but behold, verily I say unto you there were fears in your hearts, and verily this is the reason that ye did not receive."

The blessing I wanted was a successful business and peace of mind that Tim would be able to provide for us. But as I applied the scripture to myself I realized I couldn't receive that blessing because I had a heart full of fear and doubt. I would not receive unless I let go of the doubt and believed in my husband and in Heavenly Father.

From that moment my heart was changed. I didn't question or worry—I trusted. I began to build up and encourage Tim in his efforts to build a company.

I am grateful that the Lord can speak to us about *any* concern or question through the scriptures. He can. He does. He will—but we must open them. We must do our part.

Scripture study is like cinnamon. It doesn't take very much cinnamon to flavor a whole recipe and make it taste good. It takes just a little scripture study to make our whole day good. Heavenly Father knows we don't have hours to spend studying each day. He will magnify the effort we make. He will teach us and fill us with power as we dedicate time each day to studying and pondering His word.

Believe that opening the scriptures opens your life to light and power from on high.

official said to me, "You're almost there, just around the lake and up the hill." I almost passed out as I thought to myself, *You've got to be kidding me—what do you mean just around the lake? That's not where we started from!* I started around the lake, and as I climbed the hill I noticed everyone else from the 5K and the 10K had made it back. How embarrassing! I was the last one back!

I desperately hoped no one would notice me approaching the finish line. Oh, but someone did. It was the mascot. A woman dressed up like a cow, standing right by the finish line, began cheering for me. I wanted to strangle her or milk her or whatever you do to a cow that is clapping for you. The humiliation didn't stop there; a few more people started cheering me in, and then, the final blow, the announcer came over the P.A. and said, "And here comes number 74, Hilary Weeks." At that point, I put my hand over my face, ran through the finish line, and didn't stop until I was in my car.

Maybe you can relate to this. You start something that doesn't seem too overwhelming at the time and then, in the middle of it, you find yourself in over your head. At some point in each of our lives we all feel overwhelmed. Sister Ardeth Kapp said, "We feel overwhelmed, underwhelmed, just plain whelmed."

It reminds me of when the Savior needed to feed 5,000 people. Now *that's* a crowd! There is no Crock-Pot in the world big enough to handle that task. The people were hungry, but all they had were five loaves and two fishes. It wasn't enough—there was no way it could feed that many people. Even though it was nothing compared to what He needed, the Savior took the loaves and the fishes, and He gave thanks for it. He was grateful for what they had.

Sometimes we don't have enough. We don't have enough time, energy, money, patience, willpower, talent—you name it. When it feels as if we will never be equal to the challenge, we can still be grateful for the little we do have. We can pause in the midst of our need and say, "Heavenly Father, I haven't had time to spend hours on this lesson. I am grateful for the truths I have studied, and I love those I teach, so please magnify my preparation and allow the Spirit to do the rest." Or, "Heavenly Father, I am thankful that we have our needs met. We never go hungry. We have clothes to wear and warm beds in which to sleep. Please multiply our finances that we might be able to prepare for the future." Or, "Father, I thank Thee for my body. As I exercise today, please bless my body to respond and be strengthened. Bless me with the willpower to fill my body with nutritious foods. I can't achieve this without Thy help, and I put my trust in Thee to magnify my efforts to be healthy."

After showing gratitude, Jesus blessed the loaves and fishes and they were multiplied and magnified. Everyone ate and was filled. There were even twelve baskets full of food left over. (Pass the plastic wrap, please.)

He can do the same for us! He can bless us, magnify us, and multiply us! He can help us be more and accomplish more than we ever could on our own. When you don't think you can run, walk, or crawl one more step, put things in the Lord's hands and He'll make up the difference. He will give you the strength and endurance you need to finish the race!

Believe that the Savior will make up the difference — and you will be enough.

The Umbrella

I plead with all of us today, in the Saturday evening of time, to make it a priority to remember who we are. . . . Let us be kind and considerate. Let us give of ourselves and show love and compassion. Let us be examples of Christlike living and service. Then all will know by our fruits and by our actions that we are sons and daughters of God and members of his Church.
—President N. Eldon Tanner[3]

I HAVE ALWAYS ENJOYED DOING nice things for people. Not elaborate things, just small, simple gestures to let others know I am thinking about them. When I was a child, I used to leave love notes on my mom's pillow. I liked thinking that it would make her feel good when she read it. Through the years I have enjoyed baking cookies for someone in the ward or sending a card to a friend. Little did I know, one of those small acts of kindness would deeply touch my future husband.

I first met Tim in Alaska, where he served his mission. From the moment I saw him, I wanted to know him. There was a connection, spirit to spirit, that drew me to him. Since he was a missionary we didn't talk much. I didn't know where he was from, how long he had served, when he was going home, or what his first name was. So when I saw him after his mission on the campus of Brigham Young University, I called out the only name I knew, "Elder Weeks!"

I was thrilled to see him. If he would have asked me that very moment to marry him, I would have said yes! Definitely, absolutely, positively, double-yes! He didn't. But we did walk to the Tuesday morning devotional together. As we talked, I discovered he had a class in the Harris Fine Arts Center (HFAC). A heaven-sent miracle! That is where most of my classes were!

As luck would have it, one of my music classes ended as his philosophy class started. And if I told you that *occasionally* I would sort of spy on him from the fifth floor as he walked to class on the third floor you would probably think less of me. So I won't tell you how I hid behind a pillar watching the man of my dreams go to class.

One morning, after "watching" Tim walk to class, I left the HFAC and realized it was raining outside. I went to the BYU Bookstore to purchase an umbrella. There was a big bin in the middle of the store filled with umbrellas waiting for rain-soaked students. I found an inexpensive umbrella and started to leave when an idea popped into my head: *I should buy an umbrella for Tim, so he doesn't get wet in the rain.* "Okay," I said to myself, and I began to dig through the pile. I chose two I liked. The first one was similar to mine, small and inexpensive. But I wondered if it might be a little too petite for Tim. The second umbrella was plenty big but more expensive.

Herein was my dilemma: Should I get him the less expensive umbrella so he wouldn't think I spent a lot of money on him and therefore suspect that I had a huge crush on him? Or should I get him the umbrella that suited him better, but cost more, because that is the one I would choose whether or not I liked him. (If guys had any idea what goes through a girl's mind …)

I stood in front of the umbrella bin forever trying to make a decision. If someone at the checkout counter had been watching, I'm sure they would have slapped me and said, "Make a decision! It's an umbrella, not an eternal companion!"

I decided on the bigger, more expensive umbrella. It was the right choice. I like doing nice things for people, I reasoned, and it isn't nice to give someone an umbrella that does only half the job. I couldn't worry about what Tim would think or about exposing my crush. I made the decision based on what Hilary would do. And I am the kind of person that buys the big umbrella.

I waited as Tim walked out of the building and approached him with the umbrella. He graciously accepted it and we each went to our next class.

Since that rainy day, Tim has said on many occasions, that is the day he fell in love with me.

Believe that within you are divine attributes which you may use anytime, anywhere, in any place.

---

3. "Remember Who You Are," *Ensign*, Jan. 1983, 3.

The Spirit Is Ready

*If we listen and obey, we will be guided by His Spirit
and do His will in our daily endeavors.*
—Elder Robert D. Hales[4]

I REALLY DON'T LIKE DOING my hair. I was supposed to get hair that you could simply wash and let air dry, and it would look perfect! Instead, I got hair that I have to condition, comb, blow-dry, tease, poof, spray—and that takes time. Sometimes I put a quote or scripture on my mirror to memorize while I'm doing my hair. I can tell how difficult the quote is to memorize by how much hairspray I go through. This one was a full-bottle quote:

"[The Spirit] quickens all the intellectual faculties, increases, enlarges, expands, and purifies all the natural passions and affections, and adapts them, by the gift of wisdom, to their lawful use.

It inspires, develops, cultivates, and matures all the fine-toned sympathies, joys, tastes, kindred feelings, and affections of our nature. It inspires virtue, kindness, goodness, tenderness, gentleness, and charity. It develops beauty of person, form, and features. It tends to health, vigor, animation, and social feeling. It develops and invigorates all the faculties of the physical and intellectual man. It strengthens and invigorates and gives tone to the nerves. In short, it is, as it were, marrow to the bone, joy to the heart, light to the eyes, music to the ears, and life to the whole being" (Parley P. Pratt, *Key to the Science of Theology* [Salt Lake City: Deseret Book, 1965], 61).

Those are pretty amazing promises that come from having the Spirit as our companion. But how do we know if we are hearing the promptings of the Spirit or just our own thoughts? I have pondered this question many times.

I once heard the story of two boys who spoke different languages but wanted to be friends. As they played together they communicated by using hand gestures. Sometimes they would draw pictures to get their point across. Instead of saying, "Let's play baseball," one boy would hold up a glove or bat so the other boy understood. Pretty soon they had learned to communicate with each other.

And so it is between us and the Holy Ghost. He might communicate with us through an idea in our minds. At first we might think it is a thought of our own and possibly hesitate to listen or obey. As we choose to trust and follow, He whispers again. With time, His whispering becomes clear and unmistakable—and we find that our companion guides and fills us with heaven's light and power. We have learned to communicate with Deity.

One morning in September 2000, I woke up with an uneasy feeling. Tim was gone teaching early-morning seminary. He called me after he finished teaching and arrived at work. We talked for a moment, and then I told him how I was feeling; he said he was having the same unsettled feeling. We decided to pray for understanding—Tim at work and me at home. I hung up the phone and knelt by the bed. I asked Heavenly Father to help me know through the Spirit the cause of this uneasiness. In my prayer, I named each member of our family, one person at a time. When I silently prayed the name of our daughter McKenzie, I knew the answer. McKenzie wasn't supposed to go to school that day. I called Tim, and he had received the very same answer.

McKenzie missed a day of first grade and our family went to the zoo for the afternoon. I thought for sure we would hear on the news that night that something bad had happened at the school, and then we would know why we were supposed to keep McKenzie home. But we didn't hear about anything unusual—not on the news or from friends. To this day I have no idea why she wasn't supposed to go to school. But I do know there was a reason known to Heavenly Father, which He communicated to us through the Spirit and we followed.

There have been times when I haven't listened as closely—I have let whisperings go unnoticed. That happens to all of us as we are learning how the Spirit communicates with us. But more often, I try to listen, knowing that as my companion, the Holy Ghost will speak to me of things big and small to guide me on the pathway Home. The Spirit is ready. He is ready to guide our decisions, purify our thoughts, inspire our minds, teach us the mysteries of the kingdom, and confirm God's love for you and me.

Believe that the Holy Ghost desires to be your companion and that you will find a true and loyal friend in Him.

4. "The Covenant of Baptism: To Be in the Kingdom and of the Kingdom," *Ensign*, Nov. 2000, 6.

Dinner for Three

*The bridge of service invites us to
cross over it frequently.*
—President Thomas S. Monson[5]

I F I HAD TO CHOOSE ONE year of my life that I never want to relive, it would be 1997. In the spring of that year I found out I was having a molar pregnancy. A molar pregnancy is a rare condition where abnormal tissue attaches to the placenta. In my case it was a complete molar pregnancy, which means a baby never formed. During this type of pregnancy, morning sickness dramatically worsens and the human growth hormone (hCG) escalates to very high levels. The growth hormone level in a normal pregnancy fluctuates between 50 and 250,000—but mine was at 1.4 million. I felt awful but didn't know why.

Finally one Saturday morning I was so miserable that I called the doctor. She had me come into her office. I remember lying on the bed while she ran an ultrasound. The doctor knew right away that it was a molar pregnancy, and when she told us, I had to fight back the tears. I didn't want to fall apart in front of her. The tissue had to be removed immediately, so I went into surgery that afternoon. The next day was Mother's Day. I rested all day and was amazed at how much better I felt.

Unfortunately, I wasn't in the clear. This tissue, which is very aggressive, came back and started growing again. It is a cousin to cancer and can spread to other places in the body, so I was treated with a mild form of chemotherapy for three months. I didn't lose my hair, but it became very brittle and dry, and so I cut it off. It was actually kind of fun to try a new hairstyle, and that is why I have short hair on the covers of my second and third CDs.

Every week I drove to St. Joseph's Hospital in downtown Denver, where I received my chemotherapy shots. My daughter, McKenzie, who was four at the time, was my buddy. After I received shots in my hips, we would drive back home and then we would take a nap together. The longer I went on the chemotherapy, the sicker I got. It was hard to keep up with my responsibilities as a homemaker. There were many nights I didn't have the energy to cook dinner, and Tim would pick something up on his way home. I appreciated his efforts, but there was one night when the thought of eating fast food made me want to cry. What I really wanted was a homemade meal.

You can probably guess what happened next. There was a knock at the door. Sister Portee from the ward had sent her children over with a warm meal. I still remember it—turkey, corn, rolls, potatoes. It was manna from heaven. I was so grateful. What I remember most is she didn't call first to see if I needed dinner. She didn't worry about whether or not I had prepared something already. She didn't ask permission— she just served. I'm not sure she'll ever know how much that meal meant to me. It was more than just food—it was a sign that Heavenly Father was aware of me. And as He so often does, He met my needs through someone else.

Sometimes I hesitate to serve. What if they already have dinner? What if I call to say hello and they think I'm strange for calling? Would a note in the mail really make that much difference? Here is a simple answer:

> *You never know when someone*
> *May catch a dream from you*
> *You never know when a little word*
> *Or something you may do*
> *May open up the windows*
> *Of a mind that seeks the light*

The way you live may not matter at all,
But you never know—it might.

And just in case it could be
That another's life, through you,
Might possibly change for the better
With a broader and brighter view,
It seems it might be worth a try
At pointing the way to the right
Of course, it may not matter at all,
But then again—it might.

—Helen Lowrie Marshall

We may never know what our small acts of service mean to someone else. But I know that one sister's service on my behalf changed how I serve others.

Believe that the most simple acts of service are often the most profound.

---

5. "The Master Bridge Builder," *Ensign,* January 2008, 8.

Faultless

*Yea, come unto Christ, and be perfected in him, and deny
yourselves of all ungodliness; and if ye shall deny yourselves of
all ungodliness, and love God with all your might, mind and
strength, then is his grace sufficient for you, that by his grace
ye may be perfect in Christ. . . .*

*And again, if ye by the grace of God are perfect in Christ,
and deny not his power, then are ye sanctified in Christ by
the grace of God, through the shedding of the blood of Christ,
which is in the covenant of the Father unto the remission of
your sins, that ye become holy, without spot.*
—Moroni 10:32–33

A COUPLE OF SUMMERS AGO, our family
drove to Wyoming for a short vacation.
We stopped and stayed one night in Thermopolis. Many of you probably know that
Thermopolis is famous for the natural hot
springs. If you know that, you probably also

know the hot springs smell like rotten eggs. That's why we stayed only one night.

When you go on vacation and stay at a hotel, what do the kids *always* want to do? Swim. This hotel had an outdoor pool, so we put on our swimsuits, gathered up our towels, and headed outside. As luck would have it, it started to rain lightly just as we opened the gate to the pool area. Needless to say, we were the only guests using the pool at the time.

We told the kids to stay right by us while we put the towels down and the water wings on. Meg, who was four at the time, didn't listen. Unbeknownst to us, she went to the other side of the pool and walked down the pool stairs and into the water, which was above her head.

I heard splashing and realized she was desperately trying to get her head above water. It was just like the movies where arms are flailing and fighting but the person can't get on top of the water. She was going under, and it nearly scared me to death.

I ran down the length of the pool. With my clothes still on, I jumped in and grabbed her. The next thing that happened wasn't like the movies, because in the movies the two people embrace and express their utter joy and sincere relief that they are safe. Instead, I got mad. I said a few things I shouldn't have, including a thorough reprimand for not listening. In my defense, I *did* give her a hug and later apologized for not being a nicer lifeguard.

Not a year later, Meg and I were headed to Wal-Mart. In order to get to Wal-Mart, we have to drive down and up a large ravine. As we were headed up the ravine, I stopped the car right in the middle of the steep incline because a family of quail was crossing the street.

At the front of the pack, or litter, or school, or whatever you call a family of quail was one of the parents. Bringing up the rear was the other parent. Clearly I'm not a quail family expert, but I knew those were the parents because they were the only two big ones, and in the middle of them were about eight teeny, tiny, cute little quail children.

They had all made it safely across the street when I noticed another teeny, tiny, cute little quail child crossing the street! It had gotten sep-arated from the group. In an instant one of the parents (we'll pretend it was the mom) came out to fetch the quail baby. But before the mom could get there, a big, huge bird swooped down from the trees to try to get the little bird. Then the dad quail flew into the air at the big, huge bird to save his baby. Protected by the dad, the mom ushered the quail child to safety.

After watching all this happen, I said to Meg, "I bet that mama bird is telling that baby bird, 'You have to be more careful next time. You can't just cross the street on your own. You've got to stay with the family. You nearly got yourself killed!'"

Meg replied, "No, I bet the mom just hugged the baby and said, 'I'm so glad you're safe.'"

Thermopolis and the stinky hot springs and the hotel pool flashed in my mind.

Why hadn't I been kind when Meg was safe? Why did I yell at her? Even Meg knew what a mom was supposed to do. What kind of a mother was I?

Well, I'll tell you what kind of mother I'm trying to be.

I try to be a loving mom. I want my girls to know that I love them. So I tell them. I tell them all the time, every day. I give them hugs and kisses. Heavenly Father spends so much time trying to convince us that He loves us, I figure I'm just helping Him do His work. If my children know I love them, they'll know that God loves them.

I'm not perfect, obviously. I make mistakes all the time. And that is why I need the Savior. I need Him to make me better. I need Him to erase the times when I don't do the right thing, when I'm not a nice lifeguard, when I fall short.

Jude 1:24–25 says, "Now unto him that is able to keep you from falling, and to present you faultless before the presence of his glory with exceeding joy, to the only wise God our Saviour, be glory and majesty, dominion and power, both now and ever."

Sometimes I think about the mistakes I've made, the things I shouldn't have said, the things I should have said, the times I have failed—and I wonder if I'll measure up. Well, I won't by myself. But with the Lord on my side I will. One day we will stand before God, and the life we lived will be judged. We will have done our best—and we will need the Savior to do the rest. We will know where we have fallen short. We will be aware of our weaknesses and mistakes. But when Christ stands next to us, He will present us clean, pure—*faultless*—before God, and He will keep us from ever falling again.

Believe that through the Sinless One our sins will be washed away.

When He Calls
My Name

*I testify to you that God has known you individually for a
long, long time. He has loved you for a long, long time. He not
only knows the names of all the stars; He knows your names
and all your heartaches and your joys!*
—Elder Neal A. Maxwell[6]

NAMES ARE INTERESTING. You might really
like your name or you might be like my
daughter, McKenzie, who would rather have been
named Jessica or Tiffany. Oh well, we can't win 'em
all.

I watched a report on television once about
names. They said that people's names often
determine their profession. For example, lots of
dentists are named Dennis. People with the
name George often become geologists. I'd like to

think that being named Hilary makes me hilari-
ous. (Maybe I should have been a comedienne!)

I was in the Boise airport one time, traveling
back to Utah. As I passed through security I
handed the security guard my plane ticket. He
looked at me, nodded me through, and then said,
"Have a nice flight, doctor."

Pardon *moi?* Did he just call me "doctor"? I
looked at my ticket and, sure enough, it read
Hilary Weeks, M.D. I felt smarter all of a sud-
den. I mean, I'm not a doctor, but being called
one was quite wonderful.

I kept wondering why my ticket had M.D.
next to my name. So I asked the flight attendant
what it meant. She said, "Well, are you a doctor?"
"No," I replied. She said she didn't know what it
meant and asked me what I wanted to drink.

When I got home, I told my husband, Tim,
the story. He started laughing and said, "Oh! I
must have checked the wrong box next to your

name when I was booking your ticket. Instead of checking 'Mrs.' or 'Ms.' I checked 'M.D.!'" He got a good laugh at that. I was just glad no one on the flight needed medical attention. That could have been awkward for both of us.

Elaine S. Dalton said, "It was on 'the morning of a beautiful, clear day . . . ' when fourteen-year-old Joseph Smith went into the grove, knelt in prayer, and 'saw two Personages, whose brightness and glory defy all description, standing above [him] in the air.' He said: 'One of them spake unto me, *calling me by name* and said, pointing to the other—This is My Beloved Son. Hear Him!' Can you imagine how 14-year-old Joseph must have felt to see God the Father and His Son, Jesus Christ, and to hear Heavenly Father call him by his name?" ("He Knows You by Name," *Ensign*, May 2005, 109).

When I was writing for my third album, I had finished most of the writing and just needed one more song. I was working on a song called "Will

He Remember My Name?" but I just couldn't seem to finish it. I struggled to write the lyrics. I labored to create the music. It was not working.

The lyrics of the song questioned whether or not the Savior would know my name when He came again. As I pondered the lyrics and the title, I realized they needed to change. He knows our names. I couldn't write a song that doubted that. He knows us—He always has. I changed the title of the song to "When He Calls My Name," and the song seemed to write itself. The lyrics and the music flooded into my mind, and very quickly the song was complete.

Believe that your name, your life, your circumstances and concerns are known to the Savior and that He speaks of you to the Father daily.

6. "Remember How Merciful the Lord Hath Been," *Ensign*, May 2004, 46.